PROMPTING ORIGINALITY

The A.I. Handbook for Humans

BY NORTY COHEN

WITH DELANEY EHRHARDT

PROMPTING ORIGINALITY

The A.I. Handbook for Humans

BY NORTY COHEN
WITH DELANEY EHRHARDT

Washington, DC

Copyright ©2024 by Norty Cohen and Delaney Ehrhardt

All rights reserved. No part of this book may be reproduced, stored, or transmitted by any means—whether auditory, graphic, mechanical, or electronic—without written permission of both publisher and author, except in the case of brief excerpts used in critical articles and reviews. Unauthorized reproduction of any part of this work is illegal and is punishable by law.

Ideapress Publishing | www.ideapresspublishing.com

All trademarks are the property of their respective companies.

Art direction, design and layout: Sarah Downen

Cataloging-in-Publication Data is on file with the Library of Congress.

ISBN: 978-1-64687-158-2

Special Sales

Ideapress Books are available at a special discount for bulk purchases for sales promotions and premiums, or for use in corporate training programs. Special editions, including personalized covers, a custom foreword, corporate imprints, and bonus content, are also available.

1 2 3 4 5 6 7 8 9 10

Printed in Canada

YOU PROBABLY DON'T HAVE TIME FOR BOOKS THAT TAKE FOREVER TO MAKE A POINT.

You're used to giving Siri voice commands or having Alexa manage household tasks.

Thinking is work.

Reading a technical guide about prompt engineering is even more work.

SO, WE'LL GET RIGHT TO IT:

AI can do a lot for you. So much so that your professional job won't look the same in a few years.

Every day, AI developers are training bots to do just about every task that used to require using that big brain of yours.

If you let it, your originality will be homogenized. Your experiences, point of view, and unique expressions won't matter.

==We believe you have one tool that can't be automated: your Human Intelligence.==

You can use it to get the best of AI before it gets the best of you.

Do you seriously want AI to write your wedding vows?

Where is your individuality?

LET'S FIND OUT.

CONTENTS

Introduction..6

PART I: AI CONFIDENCE JOURNEY

The Best Originals Are Thieves........................22
Sample Search...24
AI Rewires The Romance Of Creation.................25
    Suck-O-Meter..27
    HI vs. AI..28
AI Builds A Better Brain..................................29
Become A Jack Of All Trades...........................30

PART II: AI EXPERIENCE JOURNEY

The Early Adopters...35
There Actually *Are* Dumb Questions.................36
    Briefing The Bot..52
Update Your OS...58
    Flip The Script..62
Use The Buddy System....................................63
    Make AI Your Personal Researcher................64

PART III: AI INSPIRATION JOURNEY

Break The Endless Cycle Of Average..................69
    Test The Twist..72
Without Human Reaction, AI Has No Purpose......76
Bot vs. Human..77
    HR (Human Reaction) vs. AR (Artificial Reaction).........78
Prompting Practice...80
How To Prompt Like An Art Director 86
Be A Divergent Ant..93
Bad Dog Will Bite. Watch Out...........................94
Wrap It Up And Break It Down.........................96

INTRODUCTION

I HEARD AN AD THAT INSPIRED THIS JOURNEY.

The kind of ad that's supposed to sound smart, coming from a prominent software consulting company and letting business owners in on a secret: there's a new way of working that will change their lives and save them a fortune...

Smart employers would be wise to know that AI can do most of the mundane HR functions they'll ever need, like sorting through resumes or writing rejection letters.

So why pay those HR people to remember what the applicant said about their hobbies, kids, or what they ate for lunch? Why worry about the human touch? It's the future, right?

THEN IT OCCURRED TO ME.
WHO WROTE THE AD?

Clearly, that can't be far off.

Writing, thinking, visualizing, and solving problems are skills that my colleagues and I know and cherish.

Applied learning, intuition, collaborating, listening. All acquired talents tempered with consumer feedback and real-world responses.

When we create new ideas, OUR human intelligence, wit, experience, or empathy comes into play. In fact, it is *play*.

Creativity, twisting up ideas to put a spin on them, is a level of permission we get as humans. We can use that part of our brain.

IT'S WHO WE ARE.

BUT AUTHENTIC CREATIVE PLAY IS UNDER ATTACK WITH THE ADVENT OF CHATGPT, MIDJOURNEY, AND ALL OF THE LOOK-ALIKE AI TOOLS AND UPDATES.

A few well-placed prompts and a logical flow of questions yield written or visual content that could instantly generate acceptable results at first glance.

BUT LET'S TAKE MORE THAN A FIRST GLANCE.

YOU'RE GETTING A HOMOGENIZED SPIN ON AN OCEAN OF CONTENT REGURGITATED BY A BOT.

Hang 10.99375, DUDE!

Some of it feels like it could be original. But by definition, it's the average answer to the problem.

Your talented little bot is surfing an ocean of the world's work and giving you the median response.

IT'S RIGHT DOWN THE MIDDLE.

AND IT'S WITHOUT A SOUL.
WITHOUT THAT FRONTAL LOBE EDGE THAT TELLS US IMPULSIVELY HOW TO TWIST AN IDEA IN REAL TIME.

Some people will like what the bot puts out. After all, everything we create is subjective.

REGARDLESS, HERE WE ARE.

AI can do a lot of things that could pass as your skills, AKA your economic value.

It could be your off-ramp to finishing the day and hoping for the best. Those out-of-work HR people will tell you certain professions and tasks may never return.

OR IT COULD BE YOUR ON-RAMP TO FINDING NEW IDEAS.

SO, LET'S COLLABORATE.

WE'VE BEEN SOLVING PROBLEMS FOR OUR ENTIRE CAREERS. WE CAN DO SOMETHING ABOUT THIS.

HERE'S THE PLAN.
We're going on the offensive before AI figures us out. We'll ask the questions.

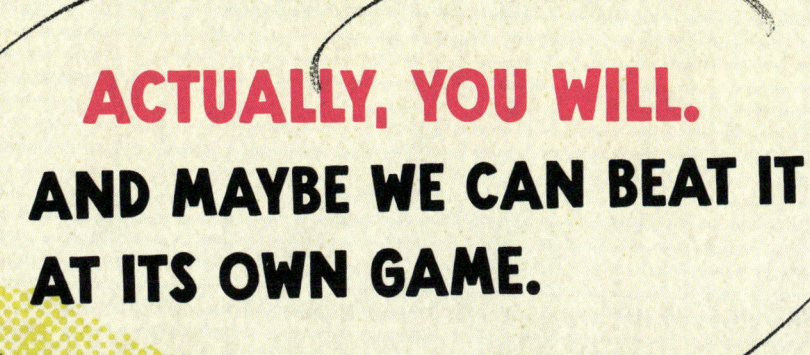

ACTUALLY, YOU WILL.
AND MAYBE WE CAN BEAT IT AT ITS OWN GAME.

THROUGHOUT THIS INTERACTIVE ADVENTURE, THINK OF YOURSELF AS THE HERO, CIRCUMNAVIGATING THE NEW WORLD OF ARTIFICIAL INTELLIGENCE, GAINING CONFIDENCE, EXPERIENCE, AND ULTIMATELY, **INSPIRATION.**

THANKS FOR PLAYING.

NOW, LET'S MAKE AI WORK FOR YOU INSTEAD OF YOU WORKING FOR IT.

It'll be best to explore this on a laptop or your phone, but you'll need a recently updated version of ChatGPT or Bing to ride along.

PRIVACY CONTROLS NOTE:

Because data privacy controls change as often as AI regulations do, it's important to mention there are ways to turn off or limit chat history and training settings. For more information, check out your platform's specific regulations.

LET'S GET OUR "PROMPT" ON.

FOR THE PAST 300,000 YEARS, THE HUMAN BRAIN HAS DONE PRETTY WELL. IT HAS ADVANCED, ADAPTED, AND ACHIEVED.

From the creation of the wheel to the production of the printing press, history's hand has always promised one thing:

THE SPARK.

GO AHEAD, ASK AI:

"What human innovations came before the wheel? What came after? Who were the Luddites?"

This latest and most intimidating disruption hasn't just suddenly caught fire.

ASK YOUR BOT,

"HOW LONG HAS AI BEEN AROUND FOR?"

"Tell me about Alan Turing and his famous 'Turing test' and how it relates to modern-day AI."

Turing's proof that humans and bots can match wits can be found in today's AI advancements.

AI IS JUST ANOTHER SPARK.

ASK YOUR BOT,

"When the internet first entered the world, what was its name?"

So when did it stop being a specialized government resource? You know the drill.

ASK THE FOLLOW-UP,

"What made it become the web?"

Surfers everywhere can thank Tim Berners-Lee for creating the first web browser and the original prompt—

WWW.

ASK YOURSELF, HOW OFTEN THROUGHOUT THE DAY DO YOU ASK SIRI OR ALEXA, OR ANY OTHER BOT, TO DO SIMPLE THINGS FOR YOU?

Bots are great for telling you the weather, reading your messages, or reminding you to take the turkey out of the oven. BUT, if you let bots do ALL of your work, your brain will turn to mush and will lack any glimmer of imagination.

SO, WHAT'S THE SECRET TO LIGHTING THAT SPARK?

ORIGINALITY.

BUT BY NOW, YOU CAN SEE, EVERYONE BUILDS ON THE WHEEL.

PART I:
AI CONFIDENCE JOURNEY

ORIGINALITY IS MOST OFTEN JUST SMOKE AND MIRRORS. THOSE ACCLAIMED ORIGINALS YOU PUT ON A PEDESTAL STEPPED ON THE BACKS OF OTHERS TO GET THERE.

So now with AI, the human creative process isn't threatened; it's just rewired. And your brain?

It's about to get a new buddy.

Keep an open mind and get ready for a Red Bull of AI confidence.

THE BEST ORIGINALS ARE THIEVES

Ask your bot, **"What are five different definitions of originality from the top five online dictionaries?"**

So what it tells us is that even Picasso wasn't an original.

Don't believe us? Ask, **"What were Picasso's inspirations?"**

Shakespeare really wasn't an original, either.

Challenge your bot and ask, **"What plots did Shakespeare borrow from other classical authors?"**

And now that we think of it, Google wasn't exactly the first of its kind. Just ask your bot **who Jeeves was.**

==Originality has never been achieved alone. Why start now? It's time to redefine it.==

WHAT IS ORIGINALITY IN THE MODERN WORLD OF TECHNOLOGY?

"I believe that [originality] is at least 90% human-generated, as technology cannot replicate our individual ideas, emotions and imagination."
—*Karen OBrien, CMO*

"Nothing's original."
—*Tega Brain, NYU Integrated Design and Media*

EXERCISE #1: SAMPLE SEARCH

There are 60,000 songs uploaded to Spotify a day. Original ideas, sometimes, but others? Not so much.

Try this...

PROMPT: Pick your favorite song (from any genre). Listen to all parts of it and break down where it came from. Here are some examples:

ORIGINAL SONG	SAMPLED SONG
MASK OFF BY FUTURE (2017)	PRISON SONG BY TOMMY BUTLER AND CARLTON WILLIAMS (1976)
CRAZY IN LOVE BY BEYONCE (2003)	ARE YOU MY WOMAN (TELL ME SO) BY THE CHI-LITES (1970)
HUNG UP BY MADONNA (2005)	GIMME! GIMME! GIMME! BY ABBA (1979)

*Sampling involves taking a beat, chord progression, or some element from a pre-existing song and turning it into a new one. Similar to any original work, it is a tried and true example of building on previous work to create something new and, sometimes, better.

Ask AI: Does [INSERT SONG] have any similarities with previous or current songs?

KEY TAKEAWAY:
Originality is an inherent blend of ideas and inspiration. Period.

AI REWIRES THE ROMANCE OF CREATION

Activities that once took years, writing, storytelling and art-making, can now be generated in a matter of seconds.

This is the only time in the book we will use a prompt starting with "write." But it is only to show you that **MEDIOCRITY IS ALWAYS JUST OKAY**.

See just how efficiently AI can **"Write a 12-stanza poem about the beauty of heartbreak."**

Fast? Yes. But did it make your heart beat out of your chest? We didn't think so.

Do you want to accept that soul-inspiring creations can be generated by machines that lack souls?

AI has never had its heart broken, it's only looked at other hearts being broken. Which is, if you've ever actually had your heart broken, **NOT** the same thing.

That applies to everything it does. And that's why:

"AI won't replace writers. It will replace hack writers," says author Josh Bernoff.

"A system like ChatGPT might be fed millions of webpages and digital documents (until) the right answer is revealed."

—JoElla Carman and Jasmine Cui for NBC News

"I think it actually heightens the need for creativity in individuals."

—Harsha Madannavar, Managing Director of L.E.K.

Think about it this way: Have you ever had something that you just really wanted to get off your chest but couldn't find the right way to express it? AI can help articulate.

Explain a friendship issue you're having to a bot and ask it to **"construct a message regarding my situation about (insert issue)."**

What advice does it give you?

In many ways, the use of AI can lead to greater clarity, creativity and inspiration for everyone expressing their ideas.

Your work, your output, and your brand are only about to get better...if you let it.

YOU CAN SEED IDEAS INSTEAD OF ASKING FOR THEM.

BUT IF YOU LET AI WRITE THE IDEAS FOR YOU... WELL, THEN YOU SUCK.

INTRODUCING
"THE SUCK-O-METER."

To navigate AI's involvement in the creative process, we coined The AI Suck-O-Meter, which details the level of artificial contribution to a piece of work. It's a reminder to make AI your brainstorming partner, not an integral foundational part of your work.

EXERCISE #2: HI VS. AI

While using AI can save you time, you may notice that it often sacrifices quality for efficiency.

Here's your first test. Let's go head-to-head with AI in a brainstorming battle and put your HI (human intelligence) into the game.

PROMPT: Prompt your HI, without the help of AI or the internet, to brainstorm five birthday party activities for a kid who likes dinosaurs and cupcakes. Remember your childhood and any kids' party you've ever attended, and let your imagination loose for a few minutes. Write down your ideas and time yourself.

Once you're done, now prompt AI to do the same and compare the results.

- **Did you and AI come up with similar ideas?**
- **Do AI's answers seem better than yours?**
- **Can you take its responses and build on them?**

KEY TAKEAWAY: While AI is a fantastic brainstorming tool, it still requires human direction, prompting, and a vision. Yes, it can churn out 10 ideas in a few seconds, but its ideas tend to follow the data it has been trained on—resulting in "basic" outputs.

Sure, this approach expedites the process. It also serves as excellent creative kindling, providing inspiration and guidance. It effectively undertakes the initial phase of brainstorming on your behalf, doing the research, and heavy lifting for you.

The creative process is there; it just looks a little different to you...

You're a curator now.

AI BUILDS A BETTER BRAIN

Have you ever heard of the game Go?

Ask your bot to **"Tell me about the Chinese game Go and the famous match between Lee Sedol, and AlphaGo."** We'll wait.

Here's the play-by-play: an AI machine beat Lee Sedol, one of the most famous and awarded Go players of all time. It "marked the first time a machine had beaten the very best at this ancient and enormously complex game—a feat that, until recently, experts didn't expect would happen for another ten years," wrote Cade Metz for *Wired*.

However, in move 78 of game four, Lee made a move now known by many as the "Hand of God." This move was so unexpected that it threw AlphaGo off and led Lee to one victorious match.

Most people would walk away from this story with a startling takeaway: AI is diminishing human achievement. We, however, have come to a far different conclusion: AI makes us better.

<u>No matter where you may struggle, AI is there to pick up the slack.</u>

Research shows that AI strengthens all links, both weak and strong. To keep your head above the water of mediocrity, you must collaborate.

Think about it this way: most of the population tends to be either right, or left-brained. Right-brained people tend to be creative, artistic, emotional, and intuitive. Meanwhile, left-brained people are typically analytical, rational, and methodical.

Admittedly, the science behind this theory is a bit dated. Nonetheless, the idea still stands. Naturally, most human beings have areas of strengths—and areas of weakness.

AI has the ability to supplement your brain, streamlining your strengths and covering for your shortcomings. We all have different brains and, as a result, need different support.

Not sure what kind of brain you're working with? Tell AI about yourself. Your interests, career, challenges, and what you like to do in your spare time. Now ask it, **"Based on the information I just gave you, do you think I am a left-brain or right-brain thinker? Why?"**

EXERCISE #3:
BECOME A JACK OF ALL TRADES

PROMPT: Find an article on quantum physics and ask AI to explain the subject matter in terms that a third-grader would understand.

Do this by downloading the article. Select File and Save Page As. Drag and drop the file into your platform and ask it to explain it in simplified terms.

If you're already a seasoned quantum physicist, ask AI to do the same thing for a Shakespearean sonnet.

Take it a step farther and ask the questions you've always wondered, like **"What if we taught monkeys to drive? What are the pros and cons of doing so?"**

KEY TAKEAWAY:
Understand that AI helps you unleash your capabilities by simplifying concepts, helping you learn, broadening your horizons, and achieving *your brand* of originality.

PART II:
AI EXPERIENCE JOURNEY

NOW THAT YOU'VE GOTTEN YOUR FIRST GLANCE INTO THE UNCHARTED TERRITORY OF AI, PREPARE TO GET SOME EXPERIENCE UNDER YOUR BELT.

Here, you'll get a taste of the ins and outs of how to wrangle AI and use it for your benefit.

You'll learn that you are not alone in this adventure of adopting the dos and don'ts of prompting.

THE EARLY ADOPTERS

While on vacation, creative director Rob Brooks took the downtime as an opportunity to explore the new generative tools making their way into his industry. He views this innovation as just another technical revolution, similar to the introduction of Adobe Photoshop.

He explains that once he started exploring the world of AI, he couldn't stop. After a few days of messing around with the model, he created this…

The photo above generated a lot of media attention at the time since AI was making the creative community skeptical and even apprehensive.

While AI can help you prepare for an interview, create your travel itinerary, or even write books you haven't read, don't give in to the temptation of effortless creation. Make sure you're using the tools alongside your skillset to help you achieve your vision.

Use AI. Don't rely on it.

THERE ACTUALLY ARE DUMB QUESTIONS

The rapid growth of AI has led to a rise in an entirely new essential skill: **prompt engineering**.

Rob Brooks compares the prompt engineering journey to getting behind the wheel of a race car.

"It's handing me the keys to a very fancy sports car, but you don't have the training and the mind to drive it," he explains. "If you do not have that, you're going to crash."

ALLOW US TO BE YOUR DRIVING INSTRUCTOR.

HERE'S YOUR AI PLAYBOOK:

TIP #1 MAKE SURE YOU'RE USING THE NEWEST VERSION

AI tools are being updated all the time. If you can afford it, the premium versions are always worth it.

> ChatGPT premium gives you access to DALL-E, an image generator, but it's not the only image-generating model out there.
>
>> Try these: Midjourney, Jasper.ai, Adobe Firefly, StarryAI, and Craiyon.
>
> You can also access custom GPTs, which are plug-ins that allow you to curate prompts and outputs for specific jobs.

While these are helpful, it's important not to depend on them fully, like for AI-generated wedding vows.

TIP #2 — FORM YOUR QUESTION THE WAY YOU WANT IT ANSWERED

Consider the style you want for your response. Then, write your question in that same style. Carefully consider your tone, level of advancement, and sentence structure.

Test it out. Feed AI both of these prompts and compare the responses:

"What are good science books to read?"

"Can you give me a list of 15 book recommendations that are science fiction and have environmentalist themes?"

TIP #3 — BE SPECIFIC

Include adjectives and examples. This provides AI with information outside the data sets on which it was trained.

Test it out. Feed AI both of these prompts and compare the responses:

"What are some good adult novels?"

"Can you provide a comprehensive list of futuristic young adult novels with a strong female lead similar to *The Hunger Games*, but not *Divergent*?"

TIP #4 — AFTER YOU GET AN ANSWER, FOLLOW UP

Don't start a new chat unless you're switching subjects. Like a real-life brainstorming partner, AI remembers previous conversations. Stay within the same chat so AI can better learn what you're looking for and not repeat answers.

> Quantify feedback. Instead of telling it to **"be less formal,"** try prompting, **"Make the output 10% less formal and 15% more engaging."**

TIP #5 — LAY OUT EXACTLY HOW YOU WANT THE OUTPUT TO BE STRUCTURED

AI has a mind of its own. If you're looking for something super specific, push it in the right direction. For example:

> **Tell me about the book** *Dune* **by Frank Herbert in this format:**
>
> Title: <Title of Book>
> Author: <Author>
> Summary: <Summary>

TIP #6 ASK FOR YOUR OUTPUT TO BE GENERATED IN A SPECIFIC STYLE

AI is trained in pop culture. Use this to your advantage. For example, ask your bot to **"generate its response as a specific type of person"** or tell it to **"assume a profession."**

> Don't take this too far. This not only prevents you from incorporating your own style, but it can also lead to copyright issues as the legal conversation surrounding AI evolves.

Instead of bluntly asking to replicate a style, describe it.

It's not **Picasso's style.**

It's **eclectic surrealism with an African art influence and elements of cubism.**

TIP #7 — GIVE IT SOME LIMITATIONS

AI can generate a TON of content in its responses. Try listing ideas you've already tried to limit the possible responses AI could give you.

Give a specific amount of options AI can generate. For example, **"Give me a list of the top five places to travel in the United States that are known for their food, excluding New York."**

Use keywords to indicate the expected response length.

For example, **"briefly," "in five words or less,"** and **"just give me the key points."** Or, just attach a follow-up like, **"Summarize in 10 words or less."**

TIP #8 — EXPLAIN WHO YOU'RE TRYING TO REACH

Include your desired audience, even if it's just you.

> For example, ask AI, **"Pretend you're a babysitter. Give me five ways to get more clients outside my neighborhood."**

You can also use metadata or annotations to specify who you are referring to or targeting. These can be tags or categories.

> Ask your bot **"[For managers], how do you keep your team organized and driven?"**

> Or ask AI to **"Explain the flow of commerce to me like you're a preschool teacher and I am a child."**

TIP #9 — AVOID CONFLICTING TERMS AND DIRECTIONS

AI is always learning. Be as definitive as possible and don't be afraid to tell AI when it messes up or gives you something you don't like.

TIP #10 ASK THE AI MODEL TO BEHAVE LIKE AN EXPERT

Ask AI to assume a profession.

> Test it out. Feed AI both of these prompts and compare the responses:
>
> "Give me travel ideas to Mexico."
>
> "Pretend you're a travel agent. Give me a detailed itinerary for my one-week trip to Cancún, Mexico, with a budget of $5,500 for three people."

TIP #11 ADD IN A TIME ELEMENT

This helps AI recall previous inputs or outputs from a specific point and not reference responses that are old or irrelevant. For example:

"From this point forward…"

"Ignoring all previous responses…"

"Since 1960, what are groundbreaking scientific discoveries?"

"As of March 2020, have there been other pandemics besides COVID-19?"

Test it out. Feed AI both of these prompts and compare the responses:

"What are recent advancements in the scientific community?"

"From 2019 until 2024, what have been the most significant scientific advancements or discoveries?"

TIP #12 TO EMPHASIZE SOMETHING, CAPITALIZE IT

By typing something in all caps, AI will understand that THIS PART is the most important thing in the sentence.

> Punctuation, including quotations or bullet points, can also convey the brevity and importance of the response.

TIP #13 PROVIDE EXAMPLES

Imagine if your boss asked you to take on a new project but provided no sources of inspiration or references. Just like you, AI tools need examples.

> Test how bad mediocrity smells when you feed AI both of these prompts and compare the responses as if you were writing a love poem:

"What would I want to include in a love poem about wanting someone back?"

"Taking inspiration from the blue sky over the snowy mountain tops and a spurned lover's angst, give me 10 adjectives and 10 phrases to describe the realization of wanting someone back without mimicking the style of any well-known poets."

TIP #14 TEST THE CHAIN-OF-THOUGHT METHOD

This prompting method breaks down complex prompts into smaller, more digestible chunks. If you give AI too much at once, it will choke.

This approach is best utilized in multi-step reasoning tasks like mathematical word problems and commonsense reasoning issues, according to Google Research.

Test it out! Instead of asking, **"Give me everything I need to know about marketing,"** break it down. For example, ask your bot:

- "How do you conduct market research to identify target demographics?"
- "What data and tools are essential for gathering market insights?"
- "What are the primary objectives of an advertising campaign?"
- "How do you define clear and measurable goals?"
- "How do you brainstorm and develop creative ideas for a campaign?"
- "What considerations are there for maintaining brand consistency?"
- "How do you allocate the budget for various marketing channels and activities?"
- "What's the rationale behind budget distribution?"
- "What legal considerations should be addressed throughout the process?"

TIP #15 PLAY AROUND WITH ORDER

Depending on how you word your prompt, AI will give you a different output.

Test it out. Feed AI both of these prompts and compare the responses:

"Give me a recipe for a classic strawberry cake. Include ingredients and their portions."

"Starting off with a limited list of ingredients, craft an innovative strawberry cake recipe that complements the flavor note of vanilla."

"Experiment with different arrangements of instructions, primary content, examples, and cues to achieve the desired results," advises Microsoft's Andy Beatman.

TIP #16   ESTABLISH RULES

AI is a smart-ass. If you don't outline a firm set of rules, it will act out. Provide clear instructions with information on the role you'd like AI to play.

What kind of outputs do you want it to generate, how would you like it to answer, and what questions should it *not* answer?

If you aim to create something original or want to avoid your output emulating an existing thing, DON'T USE intellectual property titles in prompting.

Test it out:

"**Pretend we are making a movie. Create a setting on a different planet inhabited by a new species, unlike anything we have on Earth. Include geography/climate, history, culture/rituals of the species, government systems, technology, and cultural interactions for this fictional world and species. Do not include anything related to currency or economics.**"

TIP #17 TRIGGER PREVIOUS OUTPUTS

Don't be afraid to jog AI's memory by referencing specific prompts from the conversation.

> This will be easier if you keep the same train of thought within the same conversation/chat.

Ask AI to begin with the last output it generated or remind it to utilize previously provided information. For example, **"Considering your previous output…"** or **"Per my last prompt…"**

TIP #18 PHONE A FRIEND

Not sure where to start prompting? Try asking AI to construct the prompt for you.

Let's say you're having an existential crisis (bet you can't do *that*, AI). Don't ask AI, **"What should I do with my life?"** You'll get back some sort of motivational and surface-level advice.

> Instead, ask, **"What are some effective methods for finding personal achievement and meaningful goals? Share guidance on self-reflection and pursuing passions while considering personal strengths and values."**

TIP #19 AVOID BULLSHIT

You may be a good liar, but you're nothing compared to AI. AI platforms have a bad habit of "hallucinating" or trying so hard to give you something good, they make it up entirely.

There are ways of generating your prompts to prevent this bullshit.

> For example, you can provide the bot with reputable information (news articles, research, etc.) and ask it to use that information while answering your questions.

> Instead of saying, **"Tell me about the Hubble telescope."** say, **"Referencing HubbleSite.org, tell me about the history of the Hubble telescope and the work it does."**

Don't be afraid to say a response smells funny. There's a fine line of legal text at the bottom of the ChatGPT that reads, "ChatGPT can make mistakes. Check important info."

STAND YOUR GROUND AND NEVER ASSUME THE BOT IS ALWAYS RIGHT.

Hayden Field with CNBC describes AI hallucinations as "when models like OpenAI's ChatGPT or Google's Bard fabricate information entirely, behaving as if they are spouting facts."

TIP #20 ASK FOR MULTIPLE ANSWERS

Ask for a specific number of outputs or have it call back to a certain output.

If you're working in the same conversation, ask it to **"Give me more responses like #4"** to set it off on the right track.

EXERCISE #4: BRIEFING THE BOT

Our advertising industry process starts with a creative brief, which is how we organize our thought process. So, let's show that same amount of direction and brief the bot.

PROMPT: As you're briefing the bot for whatever project* you're working on, consider:

- How specific is my prompt? Am I missing any details or important information that could affect AI's output/response?

- Consider asking AI to write the prompt. However, never take a generated output as final, even if it is a prompt. Always leave your thumbprint.

- *Unless you want generic outputs, keep in mind you're only trying to get idea starters. Exact rip-offs are for hacks.*

*Legal disclosure: While AI is working for you, it's also working for your competitors. Refrain from prompting using client names, unreleased projects, or any intellectual property and never take its outputs as final.

EXAMPLE #1

BAD PROMPT

Write me a headline for a hot sauce.

GOOD PROMPT

How do people, from introverts to extroverts, feel about hot sauce?

BETTER PROMPT

Let's describe a hot sauce with smokey chipotle and red pepper flavor notes, emphasizing its versatility as a marinade, dipping sauce, or salad dressing.

BEST PROMPT

How can you say "smoky chipotle and red pepper, perfect as a marinade, dip, or salad dressing" in six words or less?

On average, how many people in the 18 to 24-year-old demographic use hot sauce daily? What is the most common use of hot sauce?

What are non-traditional ways of reaching this market, and how can we tap into sensory exploration and community engagement surrounding our product?

EXAMPLE #2

BAD PROMPT

Write me an email to my employee about not showing up to work.

GOOD PROMPT

What is the professional, reassuring, best thing to say to an employee who keeps skipping work?

BETTER PROMPT

From a managerial perspective, how would leading business minds speak to employees about continuous work absences in a strict yet understanding tone without implying they will be fired?

BEST PROMPT

Assume some badass lawyer has been instructed to write a warning about an employee's frequent absences. How would this person maintain a tone that is firm yet empathetic?

Now, how would Gandhi react to this situation? Hypothetically, how would he respond if he were in my shoes?

Now, tell me how Jordan Belfort would react to this particular situation. What advice would he offer me?

EXAMPLE #3

BAD PROMPT

Explain 18th-century art to me.

GOOD PROMPT

Explain 18th-century art and all the factors that made it what it is.

BETTER PROMPT

Discuss the events and tools that influenced 18th-century art.

BEST PROMPT

Elaborate on the key cultural events and the impact of available tools and materials that defined and transformed artistic expression during the 18th century.

EXAMPLE #4

BAD PROMPT

Write me a business plan to make me more money.

GOOD PROMPT

What's in a business plan that maximizes profits?

BETTER PROMPT

What elements are crucial to a successful business model that maximizes profits? I want this plan to model Amazon's while streamlining productivity and profit while maintaining company values and corporate integrity.

BEST PROMPT

Could you provide a comprehensive guide on what to include in a business plan? I'm looking for detailed sections such as executive summary, market analysis, company description, organization and management structure, product line or services, marketing and sales strategies, funding requests, financial projections, and an appendix. Also, could you offer tips on making each section compelling for potential investors or partners?

It's essential to remember that AI is working just as hard for you as it is for your competitors, so be sure to protect yourself. Make sure your thumbprint is clearly on everything you do with AI.

KEY TAKEAWAY:

Know that there will be a difference between your first and last prompt. Remember that additional curation will be required before and after obtaining AI's outputs.

UPDATE YOUR OS

We asked professionals across four quadrants (creative, consumer, consultant and coder) a variety of questions to see how AI attitudes varied. Here, you can peek into each of their minds to go beyond your OS.

QUESTION 1: DEFINE ORIGINALITY.

Rob Brooks (Creative): "Saying, 'Damn, I wish I would have thought of that—what a cool thing.'"

Kenny Friedman (Creative): "Not being scared to put yourself out there."

Dr. Jochen Ditsche (Consultant): "This original piece has not surfaced in the world before."

Keren Douek (Consultant): "Forget everything you already know while still tapping into the genius that came before, on the shoulders of giants' style."

QUESTION 2: YOU'RE WORKING FROM HOME AND HAVING A CREATIVE BLOCK. HOW DO YOU BRAINSTORM/IDEATE ON YOUR OWN?

Rob Brooks (Creative): "It depends from project to project, but I have a series of, you know, rabbit holes I go down for inspiration. So I have photographers' sites like photo rep sites, illustrators, creative campaigns; I'll look at movies, [the] film industry."

Kenny Friedman (Creative): "Maya Angelou was an amazing cook and she would cook when she had writer's block because she said something like, 'There's a recipe to it, so you don't have to think. I'm just doing something that somebody told me to do.'"

QUESTION 3: TELL ME ABOUT A TIME WHEN YOUR ATTEMPT TO BE ORIGINAL LED YOU TO FAILURE. WHAT DID YOU TAKE AWAY FROM THIS EXPERIENCE?

Rob Brooks (Creative): "Wanting to be everything to everyone and therefore, they're nothing."

Muhammad Usman (Coder): "I learned the importance of thorough testing, validating ideas before implementation, and striking a balance between innovation and practicality. It taught me that while originality is valuable, it should be tempered with a critical assessment of feasibility and potential risks."

QUESTION 4: TELL ME ABOUT A TIME WHEN AI MADE YOUR WORK BETTER. WHAT ABOUT WORSE?

Karen OBrien (CMO): "I feel that sometimes the resulting work may be lacking in empathy. What I have found from my own amateur prompt engineering is that the more specific you are, the more that you can put human emotion into it, the better."

Rob Brooks (Creative): "It's still so dumb, you know, you don't get it on the first try…"

QUESTION 5: TELL US ABOUT LEARNING TO USE AI.

Rob Brooks (Creative): "It was two days of being sort of OCD, just absolutely going down the rabbit hole."

Keren Douek (Consultant): "AI was the way to breathe life into an industry that was otherwise very slow to respond to new technology."

Muhammad Usman (Coder): "It involves continuous exploration, staying updated with the latest advancements and adapting to emerging techniques and technologies."

QUESTION 6: IF YOU HAD TO PERSONIFY AI, WHAT WOULD IT LOOK LIKE?

Rob Brooks (Creative): "It's either like a really nerdy, socially awkward person that has no social skills but can make wonderful things, or arrogant Armie Hammer from *Sorry to Bother You*."

Keren Douek (Consultant): "AI generally gets personified as awkward or dangerous; clunky, nerdy, or evil. If I had to personify AI, she'd be my wingwoman."

Kenny Friedman (Creative): "I think it's just a black box. I don't think it is anything until a person comes along."

AI-generated characters

EXERCISE #5: FLIP THE SCRIPT

Thinking differently is hard; AI can help with that. Try adopting these mentalities to expand your thinking beyond your own OS and move your right or left brain to its weaker side.

PROMPT: Try inserting the different personas below into this prompt:

Ask AI, "I'm a [INSERT BELOW PERSONA], creating a new extraterrestrial coffee shop chain that will be marketed as both convenient and delicious. Help me understand the perspective and experience of a [INSERT BELOW PERSONA]. What are their motivations and emotional reasons for connecting to other interplanetary beings? How will their perspective help me with this task?"

Here are four example personas and their perspectives that can help you approach problem-solving in a new way:

- **Creative** - Emotional standpoint
- **Consultant** - Business gains
- **Coder** - SEO based
- **Consumer** - What's in it for me mentality

KEY TAKEAWAY:

AI allows you to peek inside the brains of people who have different strengths or those who think differently. This helps you understand how to better communicate with them, expanding your tools for originality.

USE THE BUDDY SYSTEM

It's only fitting that when looking for places to grow your AI knowledge, AI would be the perfect place to start.

Prompt libraries, collections of online prompts, are a great place to start. Stay tuned for more on those.

Ask, **"Provide me with five links to online communities I can join to learn more about how AI can help me with creative writing."**

Maybe you're a budding entrepreneur. Try, **"Link me to at least four online communities that I can join to continue to develop my understanding of AI in a business setting."**

However, not all AI communities are digital.

If this book has prompted (get it?) a passion for AI, it may be worth checking out ways to take your skills to the next level.

More and more great universities are offering classes on artificial intelligence. Additionally, there are a variety of AI communities in cities across the United States.

Ask AI, **"Give me a list of in-person communities and institutions in [INSERT LOCATION] that I can go to to develop my understanding and use of AI. Provide links and any additional information about how to attend/where to go."**

EXERCISE #6: MAKE AI YOUR PERSONAL RESEARCHER

If you haven't picked up on it by now, AI is the ultimate sidekick, helping you in all aspects of life. Here, we ask you to consider how you would bring a bot to a meeting, or even your laundry room.

Keep in mind, AI could tell you to mix your reds and whites… so don't come crying to us when you have pink socks. Everything it tells you is a "starter." Use your brain to fill in the rest.

PROMPT: Try incorporating AI into your daily life. Here are some ways to use AI that you may not have thought of:

- Instead of saying, "**Give me mock interview questions**," take the extra step to think about why you are asking. Ask **what an interviewer would be looking for regarding a specific job position**. You can even drag and drop or copy and paste the job description for accuracy.

- When there is a lull in the brainstorm, tap in AI. Ask it to conduct a mock focus group with your target audience to reveal hidden insights. Give AI some variation of an idea and see what it does with it.*

- Try randomly feeding your bot assistant three ingredients in your fridge and ask for an assortment of appetizer recipes.

- Describe your audience and ask what they would like to see in a presentation to make it more engaging.

- Ask AI to prioritize your extensive to-do list based on your tasks and their deadlines.

- Describe your Gen Z nephew and ask for ways to help relate to him.

- Probe for the unfamiliar. For example, **"I'm going on a first date with someone super into computers. Give me five talking points since I know nothing about technology."**

- Have AI help you with gaming. While we don't condone cheating, it is good prompting practice. For example, **"I'm playing Scrabble with really competitive people. What are ten words that use the letters y, r, and o?"**

*Avoid entering IP or internal information

KEY TAKEAWAY:

Understand how AI can impact and improve your life, especially your personal life.

It can help you socialize, organize, and create efficiently—as long as you leave your thumbprint and don't take its output as your final content.

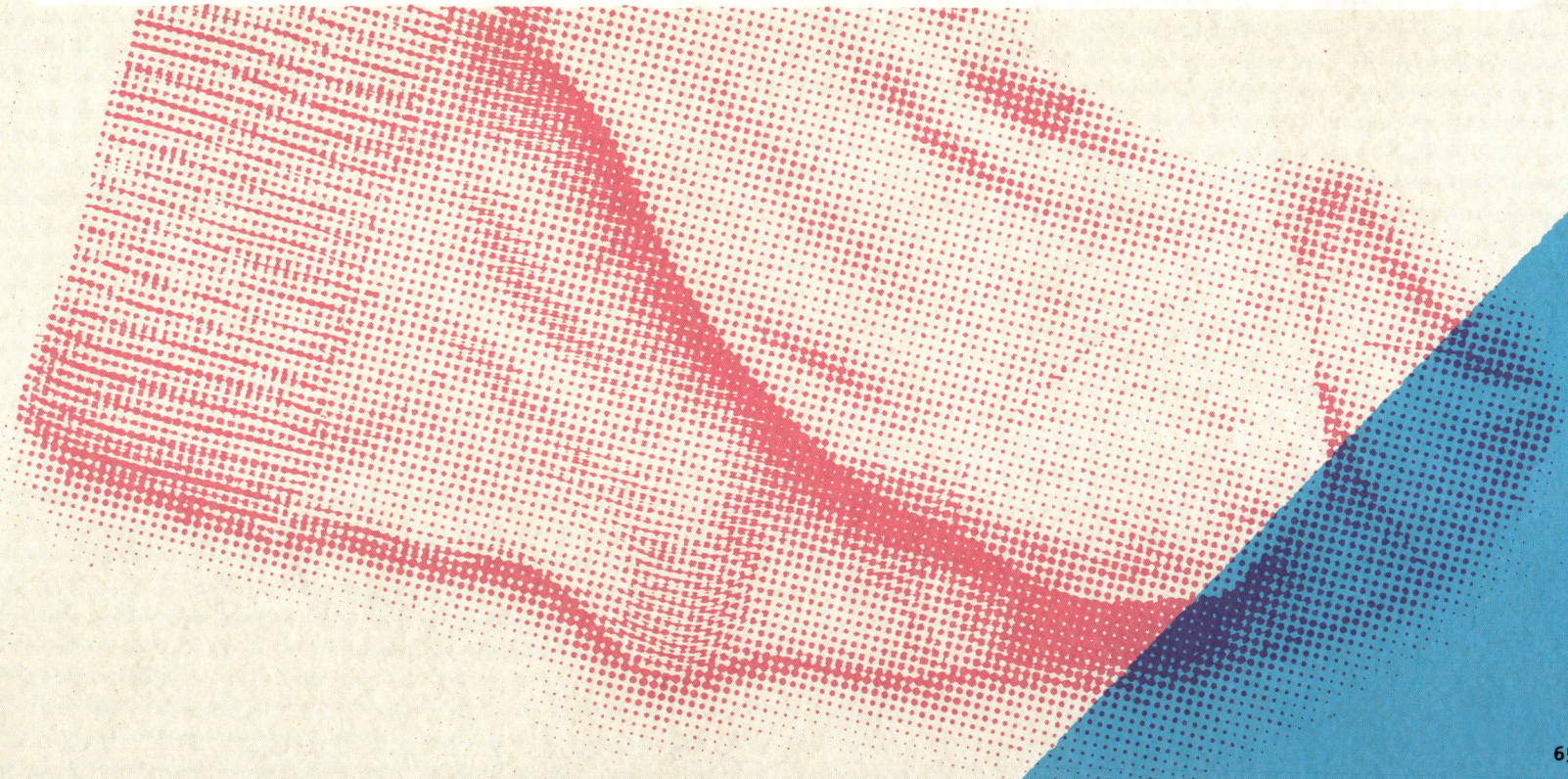

PART III:
AI INSPIRATION JOURNEY

You've braved the path of confidence and experience and have reached the final destination: the inspiration journey. Here, you'll sail through the ocean of mediocrity and try to escape without falling in.

Your lifeline? Original thinking, human nature, and intuition.

After this section, you'll have a chance to put your new skills to the test!

BREAK THE ENDLESS CYCLE OF AVERAGE

AI is essentially a glorified fill-in-the-blank pattern recognizer, sourcing its insights from an ocean of data, and _most_ of it is drifting, waterlogged shit.

Which is why much of what AI cranks out is average at best. Ask it to, **"Tell me a pick-up line that will land me a first date,"** and you'll quickly find that the dating pool is safe...for now.

But wait, it gets worse. Because generative models are becoming more prevalent and people are passing off AI's work as their own, the pool of what AI sources from becomes tainted.

Ask AI to check itself and **"Describe the AI homogenization loop (also known as 'model collapse') and the pitfalls of originality that come with it."**

According to Insider Intelligence, 90% of online content could be AI-generated by 2026. While this statistic may seem daunting, and rightfully so, it actually creates the opportunity for something that makes you, yes you, and people like you, infinitely more valuable.

So what does this mean?

HUMAN-GENERATED CONTENT WILL EVENTUALLY BECOME A "LUXURY GOOD." CRAZY, BUT TRUE.

As we raise the bar for human-generated work, we can no longer settle for basic outputs. Because anyone can generate them, basic outputs are now free and have no value.

That's why Josh Bernoff, best-selling author, gives a word of warning to those in industries threatened by AI. "AI will never replace human intelligence, the wit and character of great writing."

But don't take his word for it. Open up AI in two different windows and feed it the same prompt: **"Give me a list of four names for a cat who is white with orange spots."**

Let's guess. Creamsicle, Sunny, Copper, Peaches, Clementine, Tangerine, Marzipan?

Based on what you've read so far, how can you put your Human Intelligence to work and make that prompt, and in turn output, better? More specific? A springier springboard?

So, how do you break the endless cycle of average? Stay curious, stay true to yourself and push yourself to be better than the mediocrity of AI.

Put this to the test! Ask AI to **"Generate a headline for a local charity that gives away kittens in 10 words or less."**

You'll get back responses like **"Furry Angels: Charity Makes Pawsitive Impact on Community."** Not bad, not good, just meh.

Now, apply some of your skillset to take it to the next level. How would you improve that line?

"By combining the strengths of AI with my own creativity and critical thinking, I can shape the generated work into something that reflects my unique style and purpose," says Muhammad Usman, professional prompt engineer.

Remember, AI is merely your assistant. The power is in the hands of the creator… YOU.

Ask AI to dig deep and, **"Make a list of 10 companies using AI across various industries. Share specific success stories and challenges they've faced."**

EXERCISE #7: TEST THE TWIST

Now, you're ready to test outputs and see if AI can generate those left-field ideas that give you a spark of originality.

PROMPT: Ask AI to develop plot twists for three classic children's stories of your choice (e.g., *Little Red Riding Hood*, *The Three Little Pigs*, and *Winnie the Pooh*).

- Compare each of the AI-generated plot twists to each other. Do they sound similar or different? Are they predictable?

- Did the AI-generated plot twists spark your thinking or inspire you to come up with even better ones? How would you have done it differently?

- Be the judge of AI! Score its original plot twist on this "Originality Scorecard."

HERE'S WHAT WE GOT:

YOU: Create a plot twist for the story *Little Red Riding Hood*

CHAT GPT: Alright, how about this twist for *Little Red Riding Hood*? Instead of the wolf dressing up as grandma, it's actually the grandma who's been the wolf the whole time! She's a kind-hearted werewolf who keeps her secret hidden to protect Red. But on this particular visit, she struggles to control her transformation due to a rare lunar event. Red, initially frightened, learns of her grandma's true nature and the deep love behind her secret. Together, they outsmart a real threat lurking in the woods, flipping the story from a tale of deception to one of unexpected heroism and family bonds.

ORIGINALITY SCORECARD

REPLICATED CREATIVITY (PREDICTABLE) ———— ABSOLUTE CREATIVITY (UNPREDICTABLE)

YOU: Okay now write a plot twist for *Winnie the Pooh*

CHAT GPT: In a twist for *Winnie the Pooh*, let's imagine that the Hundred Acre Wood is actually a magical realm created by Christopher Robin's imagination. As Christopher grows older, he begins to forget about his imaginary world, causing it to slowly fade away. Pooh and friends realize they must help him remember the joy and innocence of childhood to save their world. In a heartwarming journey, they venture into the real world, leading to funny and touching moments as they remind Christopher (and the audience) of the importance of imagination, friendship, and holding onto the magic of childhood, no matter your age. This twist adds a layer of nostalgia and depth to the beloved story.

ORIGINALITY SCORECARD

REPLICATED CREATIVITY (PREDICTABLE) ○ ○ ● ○ ○ ABSOLUTE CREATIVITY (UNPREDICTABLE)

> Okay now write a plot twist for *The Three Little Pigs* **YOU**

 **CHAT GPT** How about this twist for *The Three Little Pigs*? The pigs, known for their construction skills, are actually con artists who trick the wolf into destroying shoddily built houses for insurance money. The wolf, traditionally seen as the villain, is a local inspector trying to reveal their schemes. In the final showdown at the brick house, the wolf's dedication to justice uncovers the pigs' fraud. The story ends with the community recognizing the wolf's good intentions and the pigs learning the value of honesty and hard work. This twist turns the narrative into a playful commentary on ethics and integrity.

ORIGINALITY SCORECARD

REPLICATED CREATIVITY (PREDICTABLE)      **ABSOLUTE CREATIVITY (UNPREDICTABLE)**

KEY TAKEAWAY:
Use AI's outputs as a launch pad for your own creativity or inspiration.

WITHOUT HUMAN REACTION, AI HAS NO PURPOSE

Have you ever noticed that image generators rarely get human hands right? Between too many or too few digits, webbed fingers, or sprouting from the elbow, they're usually pretty whack.

Ask AI, **"Why can't image generators produce accurate images of human hands?"** and you'll get back some excuses.

Perhaps some things are so foundational to the human experience that technology will never be able to replicate or replace them. Ask AI, **"What were the earliest forms of human art?"** and you'll find humans first made their mark with their handprints.

So AI may outperform you, but it can never <u>out-human</u> you.

Embrace this distinction; use AI to reflect culture, not create it. In industries such as advertising where our job is to reflect culture, creation is still in the hands of humanity, so don't give up your position as a culture curator.

This allows you to be more human and, in turn, more in touch with your work and its audience.

ChatGPT may be able to generate a super professional email in a fraction of a second, but can it crack a joke that remembers your client's favorite TV show? We think not. They especially can't read between the lines…

"Because LLMs [Large Language Models] are based on already existing data models, they have inherent stereotypes and biases built into them," says Karen OBrien, CMO.

She states, *"Sometimes the resulting work can be plagiarized, [and] can be extremely lacking in emotional intelligence to the point where it may be lacking in empathy."*

The differences between man and bot may seem obvious, but let's break it down:

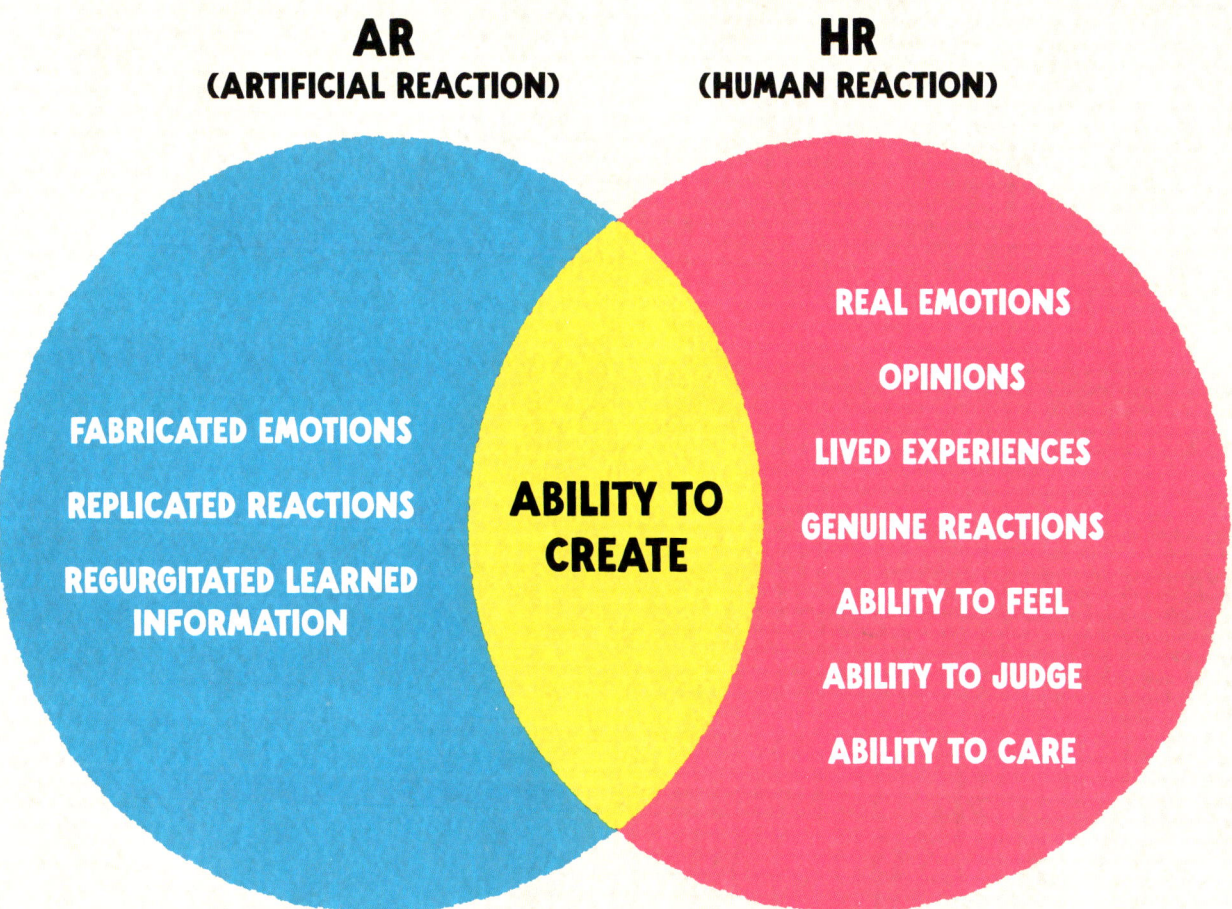

Beyond human emotion, human perspective is just as, if not more, valuable. Unlike AI tools, we can read between the lines and catch errors that may have fallen through the cracks. We can spot factual inaccuracies. We can scan for language that won't land with our audience.

For reasons such as these, we must view AI tools as just that. Tools.

EXERCISE #8: HR (HUMAN REACTION) VS. AR (ARTIFICIAL REACTION)

AI solely focuses on input and output, while we humans define ideas as good vs. bad. In a world where originality is measured by its impact and ability to make us feel, we want to show you how truly irreplaceable your human feelings are.

PROMPT: Find your favorite piece of media that chokes you up, makes you cry, or takes you back to your childhood. Something that makes you *feel*. Download it and drop it into your platform. Ask AI how it makes it feel.

KEY TAKEAWAY:
While AI can create, it cannot feel. Your strengths are your ability to see, touch, taste, hear, and smell. AI's role is to become *your sixth sense and enhance your capabilities*.

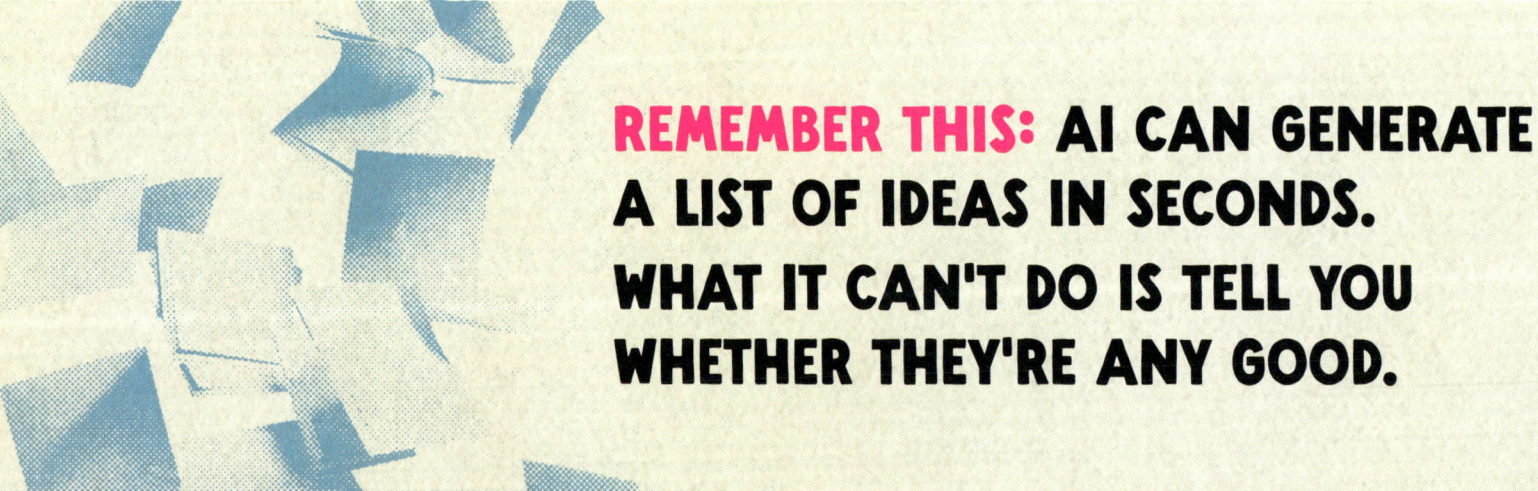

REMEMBER THIS: AI CAN GENERATE A LIST OF IDEAS IN SECONDS. WHAT IT CAN'T DO IS TELL YOU WHETHER THEY'RE ANY GOOD.

BEFORE YOU DIVE INTO THE WORLD OF PROMPTING, LET'S TAKE A MOMENT TO LEARN THE RULES OF THE ROAD:

- If you're planning on using your outputs for anything commercial, review your model's terms of service and privacy policies.

- Always include your own human touch in generated works. Never take outputs as they are.

- Refrain from asking for a specific style or copyrighted work. Establish your own voice and style before AI replicates it.

NOW THAT YOU'VE GOT YOUR PROMPTING DRIVER'S PERMIT, LET'S RIDE.

PROMPTING PRACTICE

By definition, AI will rarely throw those left-field ideas that spark originality. Here, we want you to tap into the weird and wacky, seeing if the most unexpected prompts can light your inner spark.

Pretend we just gave you a brand-new box of crayons. Let's open up your five-year-old brain and color outside the lines.

We'll get you started with ideas, but feel free to change any prompt to your own and see where it takes you. If you see something you like, go a step farther and ask AI to elaborate on any output you receive. **Let's see if we can spark originality.**

- Take the Shakespearean classic *Romeo and Juliet*, but make the characters modern people with modern issues. What would be the reason their families hate each other? Tell the story in the form of reality TV confessionals only.

- If animals were to be in charge of the country instead of humans, which animals would you place in the branches of government and why?

    — Where do humans fit within this new world order?

- Describe a world where time does not flow linearly. Instead, it flows cyclically. Tell this as a bedtime story for children.

- Give me five names for a dog inspired by Norse mythology, five inspired by Greek mythology, and five inspired by Italian folklore.

    — Which breeds would best suit these names?

- Devise a chore chart system for elementary school students that will help parents get them to school on time each morning.

    — Now, express it in old European folklore.

- Suggest convenience merchandising ideas for cotton balls.

    — How can we make cotton balls appear to be "healthy?"

- If *The Devil Wears Prada*, what other items might she have in her Amazon storefront?

    — If she went broke spending her money on Prada, what would she use her last $25 to buy?

- Create a list of baby boy names inspired by terminology found in a medical textbook. Now, create Instagram handles for each one of these babies.

- Which fictional world would [INSERT YOUR CITY] fit into best and why?

    — In this world, the iconic [INSERT CITY LANDMARK] has been adapted into what?

- What new traditions would come if Christmas was in the summer?

    — What would Santa wear?

- Which extinct animal, if brought back to life in the numbers it once existed, would impact the lives of humans most significantly?

    — How would it do it?

- Which long-lost treasure do you think is most findable?

    — How would I begin to find it?

- Give me five names for a cheese-themed action hero who hails from the American Southwest.

    — Create a short poem about their powers.

    — Now, the cheese is spoiled and they're a villain. What are 10 new names?

- If there were no shoes or socks, what would you do to protect your feet? What materials would you use?

    — Give me 10 uses for shoes beyond wearing them on your feet.

- Give me ideas for song lyrics in the [INSERT GENRE OF MUSIC] genre about a new deodorant aimed at teenagers.

    — How do I make it stand out from the other existing deodorant brands?

- Give me 10 social media username ideas that involve the word "Corn."

- I need to develop a snack to pair with beer. Help me concept new flavors of salty chips, but make it a flavor that's never been done before.

    — Now, make these flavors inspired by [INSERT CULTURE'S] cuisine.

- Imagine a marshmallow-shaped promotional vehicle. Give me five ideas for this automobile's name.

    — Now the vehicle is on fire. What do you call it?

- Help me come up with concepts for a dentist-themed amusement park.

    — What is the name, and what concessions does it sell?

- I need to convince people that IPAs don't suck and aren't pretentious.

    — What are the most unexpected words I could use to describe the flavor of IPAs?

- Develop a locker room pep talk for Gen X in a motivating yet passive-aggressive tone.

    — Now, make it under 30 seconds.

- What are things I can give to my employees that aren't money? What do the latest trends say about job satisfaction?

- If [INSERT BRAND] were a person, what monologue would they say to open a movie narrated by a serious God-like voice?

    — What inspirational anecdotes would support the monologue?

- What is the worst flavor for a beer you can come up with? Give me three names for what this beer would be called.

    — Where would this beer originate from, and what are the names/kinds of bars where it would be served?

- How can I create an authentic approach to my dog grooming business on social media?

    — What things are important to dog owners?

    — Narrate the grooming experience from a dog's perspective.

NOW THAT WE'VE COVERED OUR COPY BASES, LET'S MOVE INTO THE VISUAL TERRITORY.

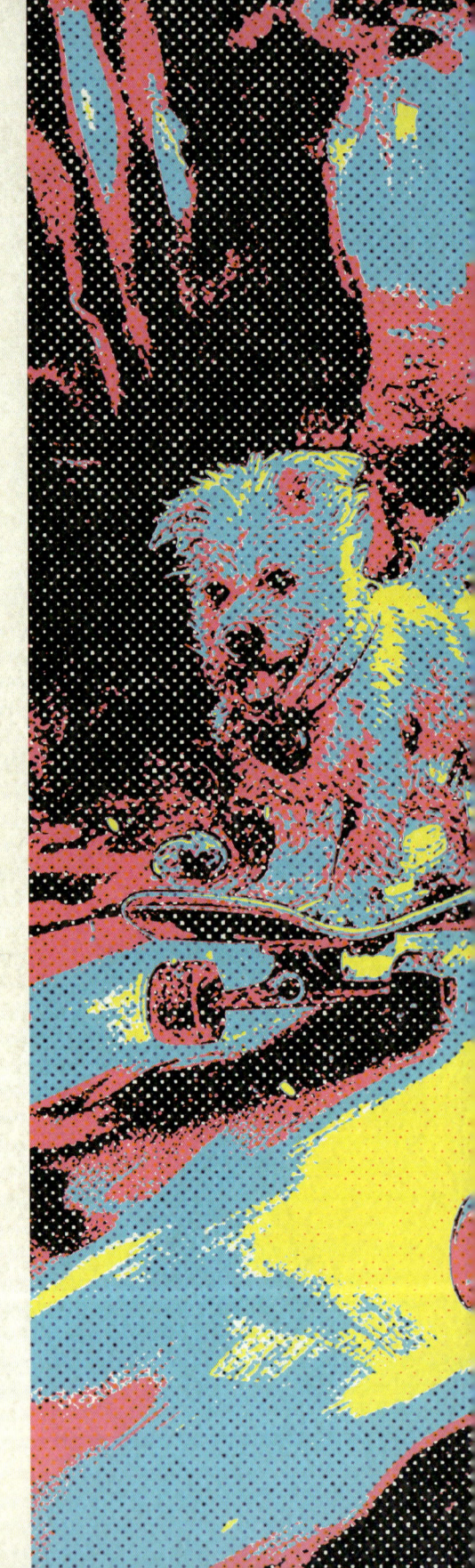

HOW TO PROMPT LIKE AN ART DIRECTOR

Depending on your background and creative thought process, how you approach all things AI will change. Coders know what keywords a computer is searching for. Consultants understand things from a business perspective.

As a curator, you have copy and art to play with so let's look at how art directors would solve for originality:

- They'll blend art history, psychology, cultural trends, visual styles, and current events into relevant everyday solutions.

- This could begin with a deep dive into the target, the market, and basic design principles such as unity, patterns, rhythm, and variety.

So for the non-art directors like the rest of us, we can respect and be patient to allow this process to evolve.

The art that is rendered by AI may be one-dimensional given all of these inputs. Applying some of these design aesthetics can keep you from falling into the pit of automation.

Art directors are more than artists. They're art historians, psychologists, cultural navigators, photographers, cultural anthropologists, marketers, and problem solvers.

With that in mind, it takes a little work to professionally color outside the lines:

- Use AI as you might a rough, initial draft or mood board, but not for a finished piece. Use it to test out many variations in a short period and save your HI for bigger tasks.

ChatGPT provides templates to guide the prompting process like this one:

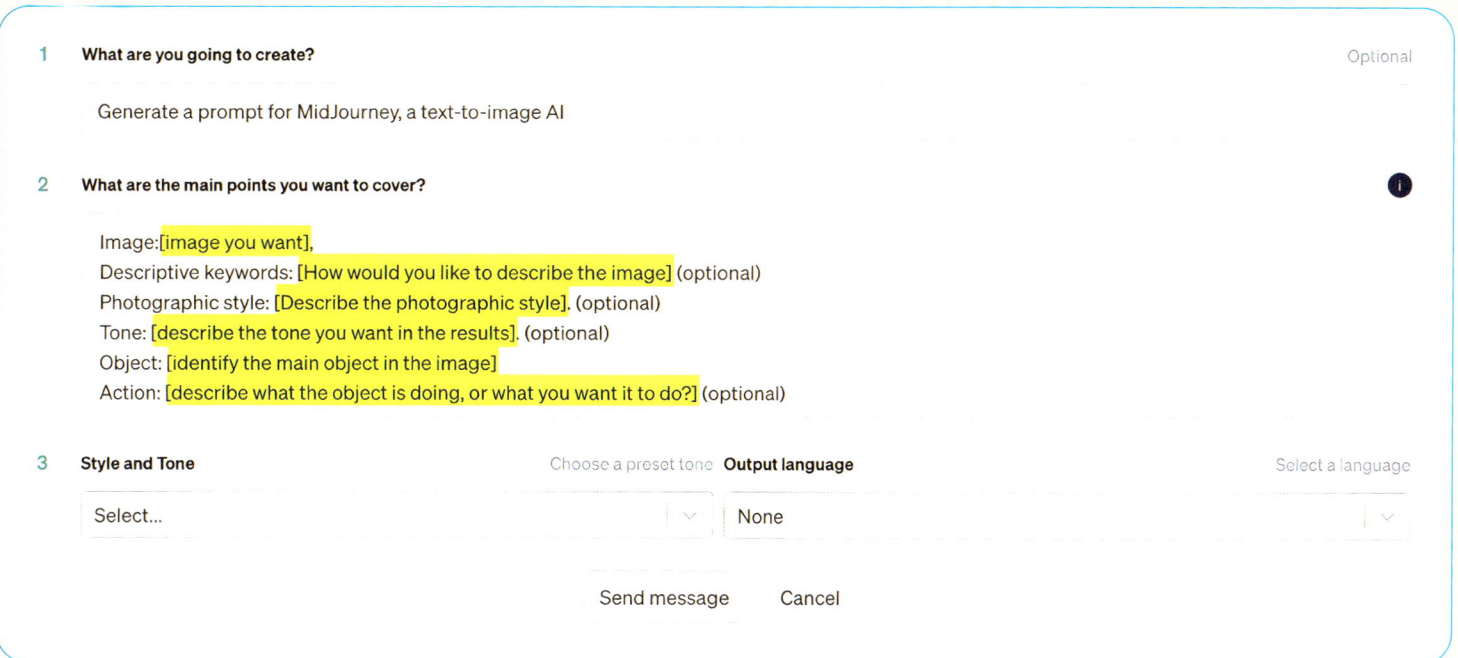

However, they leave out some key details. Here's what an art director would add to this template:

- Communication hierarchy, focal point, and perspective.

- Specify the background, foreground, all the grounds. Give the prompt, and your piece, depth.

- What type of material or finish do you want your piece to have? Wood-carved with a glossy finish? 3D elements? The more specific you are, the more likely you are to get what you want.

- Include the goal of the piece: Where it will live, the type of people that will be interacting with it, and the emotions you want to evoke from your audience.

TRUE ART BUILDS ON OTHERS. TO TRULY THINK LIKE AN ART DIRECTOR, YOU NEED TO EMBRACE COMMUNITY.

Prompt libraries are community-based forums that are great resources to help you achieve a specific style through prompting.

Here are some sites to get you started:

- Midlibrary.io
- Lexica.art
- PromptHero
- ArtHub.ai

Now, it's time to take that art director knowledge and pair it with a bot's brain, after all, the greatest originality is a combination of AI and HI. Here's how to use the two together:

First, give the image generator something to create. We asked DALL-E to, **"Make me an image of a happy dog riding a skateboard through the park."** You can see under the image how ChatGPT takes the prompt and makes it its own.

CHAT GPT: Here's the image of a cheerful dog on a skateboard, cruising down a sunny street with a vibrant city park in the background. The dog's excitement and joy are perfectly captured as it balances skillfully on a colorful skateboard.

Now give it an additional task. We told it to, **"Make the dog black and weigh over 100 pounds."**

After creating an image, click the generated image output. Next, click on the "i" in the circle in the top right corner. You should see something like this.

PROMPT

A large black dog, weighing over 100 pounds, with a muscular build and a shiny coat, balancing skillfully on a skateboard. The skateboard is sturdy, designed to support the weight of the dog, as is cruising down a sunny street. The background features a city park with green trees, a clear blue sky, and a few distant buildings. Despite the dog's size, it looks forward with excitement, its ears flopping in the wind as it speeds along, embodying the joy and freedom of the moment in a vibrant and dynamic scene.

Now you can see how ChatGPT altered your inputted prompt. It's a great resource if you have specific parts of the image you want to change or build off of. Try altering this same prompt and re-entering it into your AI.

TAKE ADVANTAGE OF THE BOT'S BRAIN AND USE IT IN CONJUNCTION WITH YOUR ART DIRECTOR MENTALITY.

However, it is important to remember that humans and bots have different brains. While we use pop culture references to communicate, AI is literal and will give you exactly what you say, so be cautious.

DON'T ASK FOR COPYRIGHTED IMAGES.

If you get an output like this when visually prompting, do not be discouraged. There are ways to get around the bot.

CHAT GPT

YOU: Make them play rock instruments but dress them as the original Beatles

CHAT GPT: ⚠ Error creating image

I'm unable to create images that directly depict the likeness of copyrighted characters, including their distinctive outfits, due to content policy restrictions. If you would like, I can create an image of an alien band playing rock instruments with a creative and unique style inspired by vintage or classic fashion. Let me know how you'd like to proceed!

Instead of asking to replicate the Beatles' style specifically, describe the moppy hair, mod fashion, and psychedelic vibe, but don't explicitly ask for it. As your middle school teacher used to say, show, don't tell.

Finally, keep in mind that no publication or client will want to use a fully AI-generated visual without your HI thumbprint.

The takeaway? AI is a tool in the process, not THE process.

NOW, PUT YOUR KNOWLEDGE TO THE TEST AND PROMPT LIKE AN ART DIRECTOR.

Here are some prompts to get you started:

You'll need one of the visual prompt tools to try these:

- Show me a rendering of what an adults-only resort themed after [_____] would look like.

- Generate a photo-realistic picture of an alien who lives on a planet inspired by [_____].
    - Give the alien a name and a life story.

- Show me a visual of the ideal influencer for water.

- A famous chocolatier just bought [_____]. Generate an image of our whimsical new factory that has magical elements but also reflects my brand.

- Show me the world from the first-person perspective of a firefly in a jar on the Fourth of July.

- For a child's birthday party, create a cake in the shape of an old-school locomotive that includes smoke, wheels, and a mini conductor. Include the types of ingredients for each element.

BE A DIVERGENT ANT

From a bird's-eye view, nature is orderly.

However, fly closer to the Earth and you'll realize that for every follower, there is a wanderer.

Picture a line of ants. From a distance, they appear to be all in a straight line—following a pre-defined pathway. But if you look closer, you'll notice that some ants aren't following the line.

Those ants who diverge often go on to create their own colonies, creating their own path.

When you're not blindly following the ant in front of you, you open up a realm of new possibilities.

Moral of the handbook: Collaborate with AI to take advantage of your ability to be a divergent ant and thinker.

From where you are to where you want to be, take on AI as your new copilot and you'll see how far you can go with the future on your side.

BAD DOG WILL BITE. WATCH OUT

Despite how it may seem, AI isn't a free-for-all. Be careful about the use of data in your AI generators.

DATA PRIVACY:

- Avoid inputting classified client information, unreleased projects, or anything you wouldn't discuss outside the conference room. Instead of using proprietary or confidential information, anonymize it or pseudonymize it (make up names) before plugging it into any AI platform.

- Keep up to date on your company's AI policy.

- Protect your information by being cautious of what you input.
    - Never include personal information such as your address, financial details, or passwords.
    - Use secure Wi-Fi and log out after each session.

- Make sure you really need AI to solve your problem. Your data doesn't belong in the ocean.

When it comes to AI copyright, the rules are changing daily. While things are sure to evolve, here are a few tips and tricks that will help you avoid any troubles:

- Review AI tools' terms of service and privacy policies, especially if you're planning to use ANY generated content for commercial purposes.

    — While some AI-generated images are free of copyright, the images they are based on may not be. Play it safe and apply additional originality to anything you choose to use.

- Honesty is the best policy. When using AI to aid your work, be up front about it.

- Don't specifically request content generated in the exact style or highly similar to a particular creator.

- If you just copy and paste, your output is mediocre. Why settle?

LET'S WRAP IT UP AND BREAK IT DOWN.

Here's a quick synopsis for your reference.

THE BEST ORIGINALS ARE THIEVES

Throughout time, the original ideas that we have honored probably began somewhere else and evolved. Originality builds on other great ideas.

AI REWIRES THE ROMANCE OF CREATION

With AI, it's up to you to decide how you will implement it in your work. The Suck-O-Meter will help you dictate your level of AI involvement. Be cautious about how you use bot-generated content.

AI BUILDS A BETTER BRAIN

AI + HI = ultimate creativity. AI can help you step outside of your perspective and see things in ways you never have. It can support your strengths and supplement your weaknesses.

THE EARLY ADOPTERS

No matter the type of thinker you are or the brain you have, AI is there to help elevate your game. It's your time for trial and error. With all innovations, we can learn from the early adopters who jumped on board from automobiles to Photoshop.

THERE ACTUALLY ARE DUMB QUESTIONS

Tips on how to get started prompting. From making sure you're using the newest version to formulating your input and establishing rules, this is your go-to for pioneer prompting. Use this chapter as your toolbox as you venture into the AI Wild West.

UPDATE YOUR OS

Peek into the minds of creatives, coders, consumers, and consultants to see how each professional views AI and its applications in their field. AI can assume multiple perspectives at once, which can help you see things outside of your own.

USE THE BUDDY SYSTEM

Lean on community, digitally and in person, to help grow your AI knowledge. After all, this is new to everyone. Working with a buddy can help you feel less intimidated by this technological innovation.

BREAK THE ENDLESS CYCLE OF AVERAGE

As AI becomes more popular, it begins to source material from its own generated content, creating a homogenization loop. How to avoid that? Embrace your human qualities as a point of differentiation and never use an AI output as is.

WITHOUT HUMAN REACTION, AI HAS NO PURPOSE

While AI can generate work in a few seconds, it's still humans who have authentic reactions, while AI's are calculated and data-driven. Embrace your humanity to breathe life into AI's work.

BE A DIVERGENT ANT

Instead of blindly following the ant in front of you, don't be afraid to diverge from the colony and create your own path. Following the pack won't yield originality.

BAD DOG WILL BITE. WATCH OUT

Know the rules of the road. Take time to understand evolving platform policies, legal parameters, and ethical considerations. Use caution and don't crash the car.

REMEMBER,

YOU CAN LET AI DO YOUR WORK.
OR YOU CAN MAKE AI WORK FOR YOU.

Thank you to McKenna Neef and Evan Snively, who helped develop the initial discovery and conceptualization of this book.

Much appreciation for the editing and multiple rounds of reviews from Hannah Boxerman, Stephen Jackson, Jessica Kaiser, Adam McBride, Sara Klarfeld, and the teams at Moosylvania and Ideapress.

Special acknowledgement to Martin Bihl for his editorial review.

NORTY COHEN AND HIS TEAM AT MOOSYLVANIA HAVE A FEW QUESTIONS.

Just in time, since AI is claiming to do just about everything we create.

The author of *The Participation Game* and *Join the Brand* and CEO/founder of digital and creative agency, Moosylvania, is serving up some new prompts for you and the bots.

And they're not logical. They're not linear.

They're human.

GIVE ME A NEW ENDING FOR GOLDILOCKS AND THE THREE BEARS.

TELL ME A LIE THAT I MIGHT BELIEVE.

WHAT WOULD MY CAR AND MY DOG SAY TO EACH OTHER?

Asking AI logical questions brings the median answer. The average of everything that's ever been done.

By definition, it's going to get old fast. So here's your cue. You can add that spark and fly over the ocean of mediocrity.

AI will do the basics. You can do better.

Since everyone can collaborate with AI to replace human functions,

HOW HUMANS DIFFERENTIATE WILL TAKE HI:
HUMAN INTELLIGENCE.

LET'S TRY IT.